THE BOOK OF

BOUNCES

Wonderful songs and rhymes passed down from generation to generation

Compiled by John M. Feierabend

GIA FIRST STEPS • CHICAGO

Compiled by
John M. Feierabend

Artwork: Diana Appleton
Design: Nina Fox

GIA First Steps is an imprint of
GIA Publications, Inc.

ISBN: 1-57999-055-8
G-4975

Once upon a time, parents (and grandparents) soothed and amused their babies with songs that were sung to them when they were children. As those babies grew up and became parents, they would sing those same tunes to their children. In this way, wonderful songs and rhymes would be passed orally, linking one generation to another through shared memories of comfort and joy.

Families today are more rushed for time and more geographically dispersed than ever before. Our cherished songs and rhymes, many of them hundreds of years old, are gradually being forgotten. They are being supplanted by market-driven ear candy, tunes that may provide a temporary rush but exist mostly to help sell this year's hot new toys or trends.

The *First Steps in Music* series of books and recordings is an attempt to preserve the rich repertoire of traditional and folk literature; to enable today's families to remember and to learn songs and rhymes that have inspired wonder and joy in children for generations.

The bounces in this book have been gathered over the past twenty years. Many of the most interesting examples, not readily available in print elsewhere, were collected from the elderly who often recalled songs and/or rhymes with great affection, reminding them of loving moments they had shared with young people in the past.

Those interviewed for this project fondly and frequently recalled bouncing a baby on their knee (also known as dandling or dinking the baby) to songs and chants. The practice of amusing and distracting a baby in this way goes back centuries. Bounces are one of the principle sources of delight in adult-baby play. Here, in one book, is the largest known collection of traditional bounces.

It is my hope that the collections of songs and rhymes presented in this series will help parents and other loving adults amuse and inspire wonder in children, for generations to come.

John M. Feierabend

How to Bounce

For very young infants, sit on the floor or in a chair and have baby lie on your legs facing you. Gently lift and lower your legs while singing or chanting bounces.

When baby is old enough to support his or her head, sit on the floor with your legs crossed with baby sitting on one knee, or

bounce on your lap

bounce on your knee

have the child sit with his/her feet touching the floor

sit in a chair while baby straddles one knee. Support baby while you gently bounce him or her, keeping beat with the song or rhyme.

While sitting on the floor with legs crossed, have baby sit on one knee while you gently bounce baby up and down so baby's feet can repeatedly touch the floor after each bounce. In a short while, baby will initiate the bounce by pushing off from the floor and using your knee as a spring. Sing or chant following the speed of baby's bouncing. When your child is a little older, invite baby to bounce a stuffed animal on his or her knee while you sing or chant to the speed of baby's bouncing.

Another way to bounce baby is to lie on your back with knees drawn up to your chest. Lay baby on your lower legs with his or her head facing your face. Gently raise and lower your legs. Or, sit in a chair with one leg over the other. Have baby straddle your foot. Raise and lower your foot keeping beat with the song or rhyme.

BOUNCES

Here, Birdie, Birdie...

A Farmer Went Trotting

A farmer went trotting
  upon a gray mare,
Bumpety, bumpety, bump!
With his daughter behind him
  so rosy and fair,
Lumpety, lumpety, lump!

A raven cried, "Croak!"
  and they all tumbled down,
Bumpety, bumpety, bump!
The mare broke her knees and the
  farmer his crown,
Lumpety, lumpety, lump!

The mischievous raven
  flew laughing away,
Bumpety, bumpety, bump!
And vowed he would serve them the
  same the next day,
Lumpety, lumpety, lump!

Jump a Little

Jump a little, jump a little,
Jump, jump crow.
Have a little care
And away we'll go.

Wee Chickie

Wee chickie birdie,
Tra la la,
Laid an egg on the window sill.

When the egg began to crack,
Wee chickie birdie
Fell and broke her back!

gently drop baby between legs

One, Two, Three,

One, two, three,
Baby's on my knee.

  substitute baby's name

Rooster crows,
And away he goes!

  slide baby down your legs

Variation

One, two, three,

  with knees bent, bounce baby

Baby's on my knee.

  substitute baby's name

Rooster crows and away she goes,

  gently straighten legs

One, two, three.

  gently bounce baby

A Robin and a Robin's Son

A robin and a robin's son,
Once went to town to buy a bun.
They couldn't decide on plum or plain,
And so they went back home again.

Robbie Redbreast

Robbie, Robbie Redbreast
Sat upon a wall.
Wiggle, waggle went his tail
And he fell into a hole.

gently drop baby between legs

Catch Her, Crow

Catch her, crow!
Carry her, kite!
Take her away 'til the apples are ripe.
When they are ripe and ready to fall,
Here comes <u>baby,</u>

substitute baby's name

slide baby down your legs

Apples and all!

Horsies and Ponies...

Here Comes the Pony

Here comes the pony,
  his work is all done.
Down through the meadow
  he takes a good run.
Up go his heels
  and down goes his head.
It's time little children were going to
  bed.

I Have a Little Pony

I have a little pony,
His name is Dapple Gray.
He lives down in the stable,
Not very far away.

He goes nibble, nibble, nibble, nibble,
Trot, trot, trot.
Stay behind and wait a bit,

  pause
A gallop, a gallop, a gallop away.

  bounce quickly

Hobby Horse

There was a little hobby horse,
His name was Dapple Gray;
His head was made of pouce straw,
His tail was made of hay.

He could ramble, he could trot,
He could carry a mustard-pot
'Round the town of Woodstock.
Hey, <u>Jenny</u>, Hey!

  substitute baby's name

I Had a Little Pony

I had a little pony,
  his name was Dapple Gray,
I lent him to a lady
  to ride a mile away.
She whipped him and she lashed him
And drove him through the mire;
I wouldn't lend my pony now,
For all that lady's hire.

Rickety Rockety Horse

Rickety rickety rockety horse,
Over the fields we go.
Rickety rickety rockety horse
Getty up, getty up,

larger bounces

Whoa!

hug baby

Galloping Horse

I like to ride on a galloping horse,
Gilliping, galloping, trot, trot, trot.

Over the hilltop, down through the
  land,
Leaping the fence to the barnyard lot.

Oh it's rillicking, rollicking, fun, it's not,
To ride gilliping, galloping,
  trot, trot, trot.
To ride gilliping, galloping,
  trot, trot, trot.

Four and Twenty

(a riddle about teeth)
Four and twenty white horses
On yonder hill.
Gnaw they go, gnaw they go,
Now they stand still.

Derry, Down Derry

Derry, down derry and up in the air,
<u>Baby</u> shall ride without pony or mare.

substitute baby's name

Clasped in my arms
  like a queen on a throne,
Prettiest rider that ever was known.

Matthew, Mark, Luke, and John *Scottish*

Matthew, Mark, Luke, and John
Haud the horse 'til I loup on.
Haud it fast and haud it sure,
'Til I get owre the misty muir.

Variation

Matthew, Mark, Luke, and John
Hold that horse 'til I get on;
When I got on, I could not ride,
I fell off and broke my side.

Three Little Horses

Three little horses riding in a row.
The first is no good, he's too slow.
The second is quick, but not as fast
As the third, who's first to make you
  laugh!

Aunt Hessie's White Horse

Can't you see Aunt Hes-sie's white horse, Aunt

Hes-sie's white horse, Aunt Hes-sie's white horse, Oh,

can't you see Aunt Hes-sie's white horse, And

Fine

gee - up a trot for me?

Don't you call him slow. Aunt Hes-sie will make him

go. He'll gal - lop a - long so

D.C. al Fine

fine, He'll make the whole world mine. Oh,

Verse

Can't you see Aunt Hessie's white horse,
Aunt Hessie's white horse,
Aunt Hessie's white horse.
Oh, can't you see Aunt Hessie's white horse,
And gee-up a trot for me?

Don't you call him slow.
Aunt Hessie will make him go.
He'll gallop along so fine,
He'll make the whole world mine. Oh,

Can't you see Aunt Hessie's white horse,
Aunt Hessie's white horse,
Aunt Hessie's white horse.
Oh, can't you see Aunt Hessie's white horse,
And gee-up a trot for me?

Hop, Chop My Little Horse

Hop, chop my lit - tle horse, Hop, chop a -

gain. How man - y miles to Dub - lin?

Three score and ten. Will I be there by

can - dle- light? Yes sir, and back a - gain. So

hop, chop my lit - tle horse, Hop, chop a - gain.

Verse

Hop, chop my little horse,
Hop, chop again.
How many miles to Dublin?
Three score and ten.

Will I be there by candlelight?
Yes sir, and back again.
So hop, chop my little horse,
Hop, chop again.

Jip, Jip My Little Horse

(Variation 1 of Hop, Chop My Little Horse)

Jip, jip my lit - tle horse, Jip and back a -

gain, sir. How man - y miles to Dub - lin bridge?

Three score and ten, sir. Will I be there by

can - dle - light? There and back a - gain, sir.

Verse

Jip, jip my little horse,
Jip and back again, sir.
How many miles to Dublin bridge?
Three score and ten, sir.
Will I be there by candlelight?
There and back again, sir.

Chub, Chub a Little Horse

(Variation 2 of Hop, Chop My Little Horse)

Chub, chub a lit-tle horse, Chub, chub a - gain, sir.

Man - y miles to Dub-lin town? Three score and ten, sir.

I'll be there by can-dle-light? Yes, and back a - gain, sir.

I'll be there by can-dle-light? Yes, and back a - gain, sir.

Verse

Chub, chub a little horse,
Chub, chub again, sir.
Many miles to Dublin town?
Three score and ten, sir.
I'll be there by candlelight?
Yes, and back again, sir.
I'll be there by candlelight?
Yes, and back again, sir.

Horsey, Horsey

Hors - ey, hors - ey, don't you stop,

Just let your feet go clip - pe - ty clop, So let your

tail go swish and your wheels go round,

Gid - dy up, we're home - ward bound.

Verse

Horsey, horsey, don't you stop,
Just let your feet go clippety clop,
So let your tail go swish
  and your wheels go round,
Giddy up, we're homeward bound.

Come Up Horsey

Come up hors - ey, hey, hey, Come up hors - ey,

hey, hey. Ma-ma's gon-na buy you a lit-tle lap dog,

Ma - ma's gon - na buy you a lit - tle lap dog,

Ma - ma's gon - na buy you a lit - tle lap dog,

Put him in your lap when she goes off. So, come up hors - ey,

hey, hey, Come up hors - ey, hey, hey.

Verse

Come up horsey, hey, hey,
Come up horsey, hey, hey.
Mama's gonna buy you a little lap dog,
Mama's gonna buy you a little lap dog,
Mama's gonna buy you a little lap dog,
Put him in your lap when she goes off.
So, come up horsey, hey, hey,
Come up horsey, hey, hey.

I Have a Little Pony

Verse

I have a little pony,
His name is Macaroni.
He trots and trots and then he stops,

stop bouncing

My funny little Macaroni pony.

bounce again

My Horses Aren't Hungry

My   hors - es aren't hun - gry, They won't eat your hay.

So I'll   get on my po - ny, I'm   go - ing a - way.

Verse

My horses aren't hungry,
They won't eat your hay.
So I'll get on my pony,
I'm going away.

So Fast, So Fast

So fast, so fast my horse can go, Oh

rig-get-ty, jig-get-ty, jig, you know. We gal-lop o-ver the

coun-try-side, A rig-get-ty, jig, we ride! And

when he needs a lit-tle rest, We find that trot-ting

is the best. We head right for a grass-y spot, A

trip, a trip, a trot! A trip, a trip, a trot! A

trip, a trip, a stop. Whoa!

Verse

So fast, so fast my horse can go,
Oh riggety, jiggety, jig, you know.
We gallop over the countryside,
A riggety, jig, we ride!
And when he needs a little rest,
We find that trotting is the best.
We head right for a grassy spot,
A trip, a trip, a trot!
A trip, a trip, a trot!
A trip, a trip, a stop. Whoa!

My Pony's Name Is Bill

My   po - ny's   name   is   Bill.   I

ride   him   to   the   hill.   It's   jol - ly   fun   to

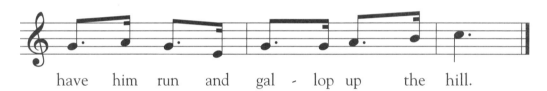

have   him   run   and   gal - lop   up   the   hill.

Verse

My pony's name is Bill.
I ride him to the hill.
It's jolly fun to have him run
  and gallop up the hill.

See My Pony

See my po - ny, see my po - ny, I ride him each day.

See my po - ny, see my po - ny, I ride him each day.

When I give him oats to eat, Danc - ing, danc - ing go his feet.

See my po - ny, see my po - ny, I ride him each day.

Verse

See my pony, see my pony,
I ride him each day.
See my pony, see my pony,
I ride him each day.

When I give him oats to eat,
Dancing, dancing go his feet.
See my pony, see my pony,
I ride him each day.

The Little Gray Ponies

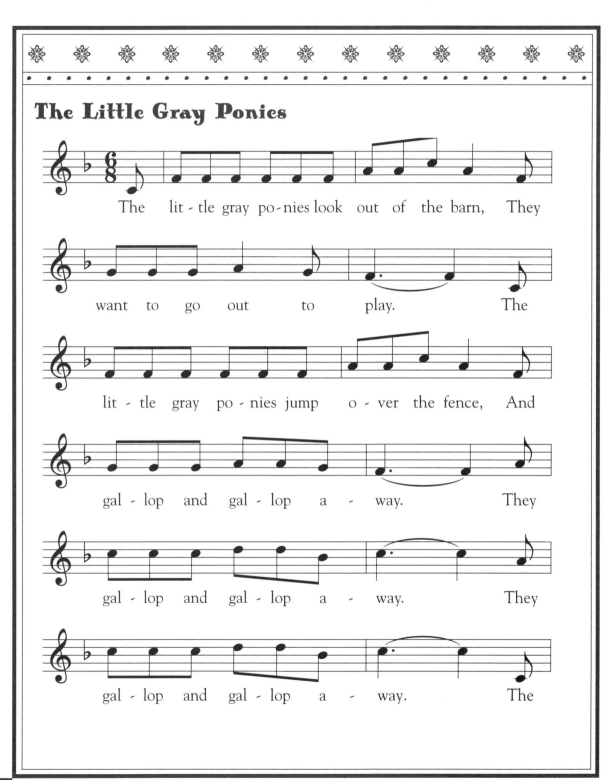

The lit-tle gray po-nies look out of the barn, They

want to go out to play. The

lit-tle gray po-nies jump o-ver the fence, And

gal-lop and gal-lop a - way. They

gal-lop and gal-lop a - way. They

gal-lop and gal-lop a - way. The

lit - tle gray po - nies come back to the barn, They're

com - ing back home to stay.

Verse

The little gray ponies
 look out of the barn,
They want to go out to play.
The little gray ponies
 jump over the fence,
And gallop and gallop away.
They gallop and gallop away.
They gallop and gallop away.
The little gray ponies
 come back to the barn,
They're coming back home to stay.

Pony Boy

Po - ny Boy,   Po - ny Boy,   Won't you be my

Po - ny Boy?   Don't say no;   here we go

Right a - cross the plain.   Mar - ry me,   car - ry me,

Ride a - way with you.   Gid - dy - up,   gid - dy - up,

gid - dy - up, Whoa!   My Po - ny Boy.

Verse

Pony Boy, Pony Boy,
Won't you be my Pony Boy?
Don't say no; here we go
Right across the plain.

Marry me, carry me,
Ride away with you.
Giddy-up, giddy-up, giddy-up, Whoa!
My Pony Boy.

Other Animal Friends

Cu-cu *Spanish*

Cu-cu, cu-cu cantaba la rana,
Cu-cu, cu-cu debajo del agua.
Ranita ranita contenta está,
Salta y come y dice, "cua, cua."

Translation:

Cu-cu, cu-cu sings the frog,
Cu-cu, cu-cu under the water.
Froggie, froggie is happy,
Jumps and eats and says, "cua, cua."

A Froggie Sat

A froggie sat on a log,
A weeping for his daughter.
His eyes were red, his tears he shed,
And he fell right into the water.

gently drop baby between legs

A a a, Kotki Dwa *Polish*

A a a, kot-ki dwa. Sz-aro-bur-e o-byd-wa.

Nic nie bę-dą ro-bi-ły, I-no dzie-cko ba-wi-ły.

Verse

A a a, kotki dwa
Szarobure obydwa.
Nic nie będą robiły,
Ino dziecko bawiły.

General Translation:

Mm, mm, mm, two kittens,
They are both black and gray.
They will be doing nothing,
But playing with the baby.

Pop! Goes the Weasel

All   a - round   the   cob - bler's bench,   The

mon - key chased the wea - sel. The mon - key thought t'was

all   in fun,   POP!   goes   the   wea - sel.

Verse

All around the cobbler's bench,
The monkey chased the weasel.
The monkey thought t'was all in fun,
POP! goes the weasel.

raise baby into the air

A penny for a spool of thread,
A penny for a needle.
That's the way the money goes,
POP! goes the weasel.

raise baby into the air

Bare Back of a Donkey

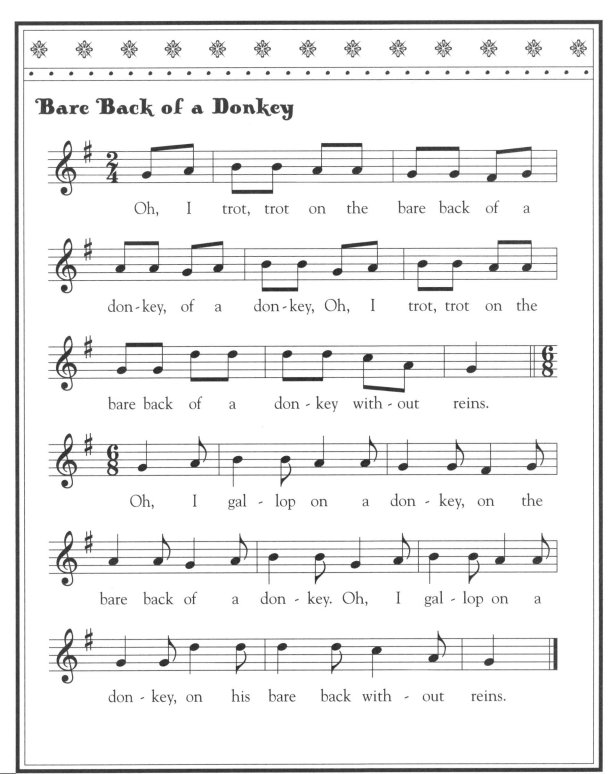

Oh, I trot, trot on the bare back of a don-key, of a don-key, Oh, I trot, trot on the bare back of a don-key with-out reins.

Oh, I gal-lop on a don-key, on the bare back of a don-key. Oh, I gal-lop on a don-key, on his bare back with-out reins.

Verse

Oh, I trot, trot on the bare back of a
  donkey, of a donkey,
Oh, I trot, trot on the bare back of a
  donkey without reins.
Oh, I gallop on a donkey,
  on the bare back of a donkey,
Oh, I gallop on a donkey,
  on his bare back without reins.

Donkey, Donkey

Donkey, donkey do not bray.
Mend your pace and trot away.
Indeed the market's almost done,
My butter's melting in the sun.

Had a Mule

Had a mule,
His name was Jack.
I rode his tail to save his back.
Tail got loose
And I fell back.
Whoa, Mule!

lean way back while hugging baby

O Misses Sippy-o

O   Miss - es   Sip - py - o,

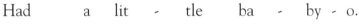

Had   a   lit - tle   ba - by - o.

Dress - es   it   in   ca - li - co,

Rid - ing   on   a   don - key.

Verse 1

O Misses Sippy-o,
Had a little baby-o.
Dresses it in calico,
Riding on a donkey.

Verse 2

O Mrs. Epplewhite,
Are you coming out tonight?
You look such a bonny sight,
Riding on a donkey.

Reindeer Go *Norwegian*

Rein - deer go o'er the snow, Fast,

fast and nev - er slow. Up and down,

through the town. Good rein-deer go, go, go!

Verse 1

Reindeer go o'er the snow,
Fast, fast and never slow.
Up and down, through the town.
Good reindeer go, go, go!

Verse 2

Reindeer fly 'neath the sky,
Where starlets twinkle high.
O'er the hill, smooth and still.
Good reindeer fly, fly, fly!

Great A

Great A,
Little A,
Bouncing B!
The cat's in the cupboard
And can't see me.

cover baby's eyes for peek-a-boo

Little Johnny Morgan

Little Johnny Morgan,
Gentleman of Wales,
Came riding on a nanny-goat,
Smelling of pigs' tails.

Katie Beardie

Katie Beardie had a cow,
Black and white about the mouth.
Wasn't that a dainty cow?
Dance, Katie Beardie.

Katie Beardie had a hen,
Cackled but and cackled ben.
Wasn't that a dainty hen?
Dance, Katie Beardie.

Katie Beardie had a cock,
That could spin, and bake and rock.
Wasn't that a dainty cock?
Dance, Katie Beardie.

Katie Beardie had a grice,
It could skate upon the ice.
Wasn't that a dainty grice?
Dance, Katie Beardie.

There Was a Little Grasshopper

There was a little grasshopper,
Always on the jump.
Because he never looked ahead,
He always went Bump!

gently drop baby between legs

Going Places...

Up the Wooden Hill

Up the wooden hill to blanket fair,
What shall we have when we get
  there?
A bucketful of water
  and a penny worth of hay,
Gee up, Dobbin! All the way.

Chick! My Naggie

Chick! my naggie,
Chick! my naggie,
How many miles to Aberdaigy?
Eight and eight and another eight,
Try to win them by candlelight.

Quick to the Market

Quick to the market, Jenny come trot,
Spilt all the buttermilk, every cup.
Every drop and every dram,
Jenny came home with an empty can.

As I Was Going to Banbury

As I was going to Banbury
All on a summer day.
My wife had butter, eggs and cheese
And I had corn and hay.
Bob drove the kine and Tom the swine,
Dick led the foal and mare;
I sold them all, then home again
We came from Banbury Fair.

Come Up, My Horse

Come up, my horse, to Budleigh Fair.
What shall we have when we get there?

Sugar and figs and elecampane;[*]
Home again, home again, master and
  dame.

[*] *a tall, coarse plant used medicinally*

Variation

Gee up, my horse, to Budleigh Fair.
What shall we do when we get there?
Candy and fruits and red sugar balls,
'Round about riding and coconut stalls.

From Wibbleton to Wobbleton

From Wibbleton to Wobbleton is
fifteen miles,
three fast bounces on "fifteen miles"
From Wobbleton to Wibbleton is
fifteen miles,
three fast bounces on "fifteen miles"
From Wibbleton to Wobbleton,
From Wobbleton to Wibbleton,
From Wibbleton to Wobbleton is
fifteen miles.
three fast bounces on "fifteen miles"

The Meadow-bout Fields

Oh, I have been to the
meadow-bout fields,
And I have been to the gorses.
Oh, I have been to the
meadow-bout fields,
To seek my master's horses.
And I got wet and very, very wet,
And I got wet and weary,
And I got wet and very, very wet,
When I came home to Mary.

I Came to the River

I came to the river
and I couldn't get across,
Paid five dollars for an old blind horse.
Wouldn't go ahead,
nor he wouldn't stand still,
So he went up and down
like an old saw mill.

Now Rocking Horse, Rocking Horse

Now rocking horse, rocking horse,
where shall we go?
The world's such a very big place,
you must know.
"To see all its wonders," the wise
people say,
"'Twould take us together
a year and a day."

Here in the Morning

Here in the morning
  we're starting so soon,
Give us a message,
  we'll ride to the moon.
Straight through the meadows and
  hop o'er the stile,
And we will but charge
  a farthing a mile.
A farthing a mile! A farthing a mile!
We will but charge you
  a farthing a mile.

I'm a Butcher

I'm a butcher and you're a butcher,
To market, to buy a cow, we'll go.
You'll pay the money,
  I'll do the talking,
With pretty maids all in a row.

Cripple Dick

Cripple Dick upon a stick,
Sandy on a soo.
Ride away to Galloway,
To buy a pound of woo.

Variation

Richard Dick upon a stick,
Sampson on a sow,
We'll ride away to Colley Fair,
To buy a horse to plow.

Mammy, Daddy

Mammy, Daddy, Uncle Dick,
Went to Dublin on a stick.
Stick broke, what a joke,
Mammy, Daddy, Uncle Dick.

Variation

Mother and Father and Uncle Dick,
Went to London on a stick.
The stick broke and made a smoke,
And stiffled all the London folk.

There Was an Old Woman

There was an old woman,
As I have heard tell,
She went to sell pies,
But her pies would not sell.

She hurried back home,
But her step was too high,
lift baby up high
And she stumbled and fell,
gently lower baby between legs
And a dog ate her pie.
gently tickle baby

Ride a Cock-Horse

Ride a cock-horse to Banbury Cross,
To see a fine lady upon a white horse.
Rings on her fingers and bells on her
   toes,
She shall have music wherever she
   goes.

Variation 1

Ride a cock-horse to Banbury Cross,
To buy little Johnny a galloping
   horse.
It trots behind and ambles before
And Johnny shall ride
   'til he can ride no more.

Variation 2

Ride a cock-horse to Banbury Cross,
To see what Tommy can buy.
A penny white loaf,
   a penny white cake
And a two-penny apple pie.

Variation 3

Ride a little pony to Banbury Cross,
See the great lady on the white horse.
Rings on her fingers, bells on her toes,
Whooooops ol' Dolly, and away we go!

gently lower baby between your legs and lift baby

up again

Variation 4

Ride a white mare to Banbury Fair,
To see what a penny will buy.
A farthing for cake
   and a farthing for ale
And a ha' penny apple pie.

To Market, to Market

To market, to market, to buy a fat pig,
Home again, home again, jiggity jig.

To market, to market, to buy a fat hog,
Home again, home again, jiggity jog.

To market, to market,
  to buy a plum bun,
Home again, home again,
  market is done.

Grandfather, Grandfather

Grandfather, grandfather,
  show your delight,
In comes Betty all in white.
White shoes and stockings,
  white curly hair;
Isn't she a pretty girl to take
  to the fair?

Upon a Cock Horse

Upon a cock horse to market I'll trot,
To buy a pig to boil in the pot.
A shilling a quarter, a crown a side,
If it had not been killed,
  it would surely have died.

Variation

To market, to market, a gallop, a trot,
To buy some good mutton
  to put in the pot.
Three pennies a quarter, a dollar a side,
If it hadn't been killed,
  it soon would have died.

Here We Go

Here we go, here we go, go-ing to town To

get my old shoe lined and bound.

Old hare hip and old hare hop and

old hare eat my tur - nip top.

Verse

Here we go, here we go, going to town
To get my old shoe lined and bound.
Old hare hip and old hare hop
And old hare eat my turnip top.

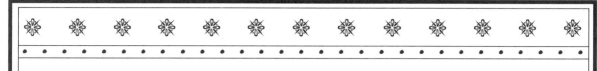

Trip a Trop a Tronjes

Trip a trop a Tron - jes, Up and down and

o - ver; The pigs are in the bean patch, The

cows are in the clo - ver. The ducks are in the

wa - ter place, The calf is in the long grass;

So big my ba - by is, Po - pa yeh vah.

Verse

Trip a trop a Tronjes,
Up and down and over;
The pigs are in the bean patch,
The cows are in the clover.

The ducks are in the water place,
The calf is in the long grass;
So big my baby is,
Popa yeh vah.

Were You Ever in Québec?

Were you ev-er in Qué-bec, Stow-ing tim-ber

on the deck, Where there's a king with a gold-en crown,

Rid-ing on a don-key? Hey, ho, a-

way we go, Don-key rid-ing, don-key rid-ing,

Hey, ho, a-way we go, Rid-ing on a don-key.

Verse

Were you ever in Québec,
Stowing timber on a deck,
Where there's a king
  with a golden crown,
Riding on a donkey?

Hey, ho, away we go,
Donkey riding, donkey riding,
Hey, ho, away we go,
Riding on a donkey.

Giddy Up!...

Giddy Up Neddy

Giddy up <u>Neddy</u>, to the fair;

substitute baby's name

What shall we buy when we get there?
A penny for an apple
 and a penny for a pear;
Giddy up Neddy, to the fair.

Giddy Up Horsie

Giddy up horsie,
Go to town,
Take little <u>Shirley</u> down to town.

substitute baby's name

Whoa, horsie!
Whoa, horsie!

slide child down your legs

Giddy Up

Giddy up,

with legs crossed, have baby sit on your foot

Giddy up,
Giddy up,
Whoa!

pull baby up by the arms

Gitty Up, Gitty Up

Gitty up, gitty up,
Gitty, horsey.
Gitty up, gitty up,
Gitty up, go!

lift baby up high

Slow down, slow down,
Slow down, horsey.
Slow down, slow down,
Horsey, whoa!

lean way back holding baby

Gitty Up Napoleon

Git - ty up Na - po - le - on, it looks like rain.

Git - ty up Na - po - le - on, it looks like rain.

I'll be durned if the but - ter ain't churned.

Git - ty up Na - po - le - on, it looks like rain.

Verse

Gitty up Napoleon, it looks like rain.
Gitty up Napoleon, it looks like rain.
I'll be durned if the butter ain't churned.
Gitty up Napoleon, it looks like rain.

straighten legs and let baby slide down

Gee Up

Gee up, gee up, lit - tle horse, You don't cost a

pen - ny worth. While the chil - dren still are small,

Hob - by horse is best of all. When they're big and

bon - ny, A horse they'll ride or po - ny. Trit, trit, trot, we're

off to town, One, two, three, you all fall down!

Verse

Gee up, gee up, little horse,
You don't cost a penny worth.
While the children still are small,
Hobby horse is best of all.

When they're big and bonny,
A horse they'll ride or pony.
Trit, trit, trot, we're off to town,
One, two, three, you all fall down!

gently drop baby between your legs

Gee Up, Run Along

Gee up, run a-long, Gee up, run a-long,

Gee up, run a-long, Whoa, stop, whoa!

Verse

Gee up, run along,
Gee up, run along,
Gee up, run along,
Whoa, stop, whoa!

Hippety Hop!

Hoppe, Hoppe Reiter (Hop, Hop Rider) *German*

Hoppe, hoppe Reiter,
  wenn er fällt dann schreit er!

bounce baby on knee

Fällt er in den Graben,
  fressen ihn die Raben.

lay baby on his/her back and pick him/her up

again

Fällt er in den Sumpf,
  Macht der Reiter plumps.

gently lower baby to the ground

Translation:

Hop, hop rider,
  when he falls, he yells!
When he falls into the ditch,
  Ravens come and bite him.
When he falls into the swamp,
  The rider makes a splash.

Variation

Hoppe, hoppe Reiter,
  wenn er fällt dann schreit er!

bounce baby on knee

Fällt er in den Graben?
Fällt er in den Dreck?

lay baby on his/her back and pick him/her up

again

Dann-BUMS ist er weg!
Dann-BUMS ist er weg!

gently lower baby to the ground, lift baby up,

then lower baby again

Translation:

Hop, hop rider,
  When he falls, he yells!
Will he fall in the ditch?
Will he fall in the mud?
Then BOOM he is gone!
Then BOOM he is gone!

Hippety Hop to Bed

Hippety hop to bed,
I'd rather stay up instead,
But when mother says "must,"
There is nothing but "Just,

pause

Go hippety hop to bed."

quicker bounces

Handy Spandy

Han - dy Span - dy, Jack - o Dan - dy,

Loves plum cake and su - gar can - dy, He

bought some at the cor - ner shop, And

home he came hop, hop, hop.

Verse

Handy Spandy, Jack-o Dandy,
Loves plum cake and sugar candy,
He bought some at the corner shop,
And home he came hop, hop, hop.

Hippity Hop to the Candy Shop

Hip - pi - ty hop to the can - dy shop, To

buy our - selves some can - dy.

Some for you and some for me, And

some for sis - ter Man - dy.

Verse

Hippity hop to the candy shop,
To buy ourselves some candy.
Some for you and some for me,
And some for sister Mandy.

Spoken Variation 1

Hippity hop to the barber shop,
To buy a stick of candy.
One for you and one for me,
And one for Dicky Dandy.

Spoken Variation 2

Hippity hop to the sweetie shop,
To buy a stick of candy.
One for you and one for me,
And one for sister Mandy.

Spoken Variation 3 *(a Scottish bounce)*

Little horsey go to town,
Buy a bag of candy.
One for you and one for me,
And one for sister Sandy/brother Andy.

Spoken Variation 4

Trotty horsey went to town,
To get some sugar cake and candy.
Some for you and some for me,
And some for sister Frannie.
Look out horsey, Don't fall down!

gently lower baby between legs

Me and My Horse

Me and my horse go hip - pi - ty,
hop - pi - ty, Me and my horse go
clip - pi - ty, clop - pi - ty, As we go
rid - ing jig - gi - ty, jog - gi - ty,
O - ver the roll - ing plain.

Verse

Me and my horse go hippity, hoppity,
Me and my horse go clippity, cloppity,
As we go riding jiggity, joggity,
Over the rolling plain.

Trit Trot!

A Trot and a Canter

A trot and a canter,
A gallop and over.
Out of the saddle
And roll in the clover.

Trot, Trot, Jolt

Trot, trot, jolt!
The farmer has a colt.
The colt he runs away,
The farmer falls, hooray!

gently drop baby between legs
Bump! Goes the farmer!

lift baby up high

Trot, Trot Horsie

Trot, trot horsie,
Going way to Fife.
Coming back on Monday
With a new wife.

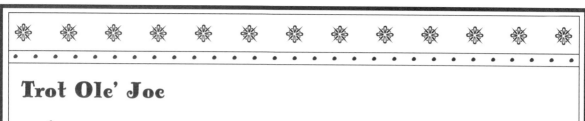

Trot Ole' Joe

Trot Ole' Joe, Trot Ole' Joe, You ride bet-ter'n an-y

horse I know. Trot Ole' Joe, Trot Ole' Joe,

You're the best horse in the coun-try - o.

Verse

Trot Ole' Joe, Trot Ole' Joe,
You ride better'n any horse I know.
Trot Ole' Joe, Trot Ole' Joe,
You're the best horse in the country-o.

Hopp, Hopp, Hopp (Trot, Trot, Trot) *German*

Hopp, hopp, hopp, Pferd - chen lauf Ga -
Trot, trot, trot, Go and nev - er

lopp. Ü - ber Stock und ü - ber Steine,
stop. Trudge a - long my lit - tle po - ny,

A - ber brich dir nicht die Beine. Im - mer im Ga -
Where 'tis rough and where 'tis sto - ny. Trot, trot, trot, trot,

lopp, Hopp, hopp, hopp, hopp, hopp.
trot, Go and nev - er stop.

Verse

Hopp, hopp, hopp,
Pferdchen lauf Galopp.
Über Stock und über Steine,
Aber brich dir nichct die Beine.
Immer im Galopp,
Hopp, hopp, hopp, hopp, hopp.

the book of bounces

Translation:

Trot, trot, trot,
Go and never stop.
Trudge along my little pony,
Where 'tis rough and where 'tis stony.
Trot, trot, trot, trot, trot,
Go and never stop.

Verse 2

Trot, trot, trot!
Little horse, gallop!
Over sticks and stones
But don't break your bones!
Trot, trot, trot, trot, trot!
Little horse, gallop!

Trot, Trot, Pony Trot

Trot, trot, po-ny trot! Trot to Grand-ma's gate - way.

She'll come out and call her dog, And then we'll ride on

jog - a - jog. Trot, trot, po-ny trot! Trot, trot, po-ny trot!

Verse

Trot, trot, pony trot!
Trot to Grandma's gateway.
She'll come out and call her dog,
And then we'll ride on jog-a-jog.
Trot, trot, pony trot!
Trot, trot, pony trot!

Trot, Trot to Boston...

Trot, Trot to Boston

Trot, trot to Boston,
On a loaf of bread.
Trot, trot home again,
The old horse is dead.

Variation 1

Trot, trot to Boston,
To buy a fat pig.
Home again, home again,
Joggity jig.

Variation 2

Trot, trot to Boston,
Trot, trot to Lynn.
You better be careful
Or you might fall in!

gently drop baby between your legs

Variation 3

Trot, trot to Boston,
Trot, trot to Lynn.
Trot, trot home again
But don't fall in!

Variation 4

Trit, trot to Boston,
Trit, trot to Lynn.
Take care little boy
You don't fall in!

Variation 5

Ride the train to Boston,
Ride the train to Lynn.
Be careful when you get there,
You don't fall in!

Trot On to Boston

Trot on to Boston on the old mare,
Going to get baby a sweet, sweet pear.
When we got there, the tree was bare.
Had to go all the way back home
  again.
Limp, hop, limp, hop, limp, hop!

alternate pushing and pulling baby's arms like a locomotive

Trot, Trot to Boston Town

(Variation of Hippity Hop to the Candy Shop)

Trot, trot to Bos - ton town To buy a stick of can - dy.

One for you and one for me and one for Dick - y Dan - dy.

Verse

Trot, trot to Boston town
To buy a stick of candy.
One for you and one for me
And one for Dicky Dandy.

Riding Along...

Ride Away, Ride Away

Ride away, ride away, <u>baby</u> shall ride,

substitute baby's name

And she shall have pussy cat
  tied to one side,
And she shall have little dog
  tied to the other
And baby shall ride to see
  her Grandmother.

Variation 1

Ride away, ride away, <u>baby</u> shall ride,

substitute baby's name

And have a wee puppy dog
  tied to one side,
A wee puss-cat shall be
  tied to the other
And baby shall ride to see his/her
  Grandmother.

Variation 2

Off we go to London,
  to London we shall ride.

Little dog and kitty cat tied to a side.
Little dog on one side,
  and kitty on the other,
And away we shall go to see
  Grandmother.

Ride a Horsey

Ride, ride a horsey,
Everybody's gone away.
Bring Daddy home a pretzel,
When he comes home today!

So Ride the Children

So ride, so ride the children,
When they still are wee.
When they're older, then of course,
They will ride upon a horse.
Ride to lands beyond the seas,
Where pretty maidens grow on trees!
If I had thought of that before,
I'd have brought one to your door!

Here Come Three Kings

Here come three kings a rid - ing, A

rid - ing, a rid - ing. Here come three kings a

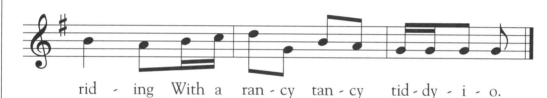

rid - ing With a ran - cy tan - cy tid - dy - i - o.

Verse

Here come three kings a riding,
A riding, a riding.
Here come three kings a riding
With a rancy tancy tiddy-i-o.

Rida, Rida (Ride and Ride) *Swedish*

Ri - da, ri - da, ran - ke, Häs - ten het - er
Rid - ing, rid - ing, rid - ing, The horse's name is

Blan - ka. Vart skall vi ri - da?
Blan - ka. Where shall we ride to? To

Till en lit - en pig - a. Vad skall hon het -
see a lit - tle la - dy. What will her name

a? Söt - a Mar - gar - e - a.
be? Pret - ty Mar - gar - e - ta.

Verse

Rida, rida, ranka,
Hästen heter Blanka.
Vart skall vi rida?
Till en liten piga.
Vad skall hon heta?
Söta Margareta

Translation:

Riding, riding, riding,
The horse's name is Blanka.
Where shall we ride to?
To see a little lady.
What will her name be?
Pretty Margareta.

Ride a Horsey

Ride a hors - ey up and down.

Ride a hors - ey, ride to town.

Verse

Ride a horsey up and down.
Ride a horsey, ride to town.

Ride, Charley, Ride

Ride, Char-ley, ride. Ride that hors-ey, ride!

Verse

Ride, Charley, ride.
Ride that horsey, ride!

Ride and Ride the Pony

Ride and ride the po - ny, A mile an hour on - ly.

Jump o - ver the tree stump, Down falls the ba - by.

Verse 1

Ride and ride the pony,
A mile an hour only.
Jump over the tree stump,
Down falls the baby.

Verse 2

Ride and ride the pony,
A mile an hour only.
Jump over the hill,
Baby takes a spill.

Ride Away on Your Horses

Ride   a - way on your hors - es, your hors - es, your

hors - es.   Ride   a - way on your hors - es   Ride

on,   Ride   on.   Gal - lop - ing gal - lop - ing

gal - lop - ing gal - lop - ing,   on   we   go,   oh,

Ride   a - way on your hors - es your hors - es your hors - es.

Ride   a - way on your hors - es, Now Whoa! Whoa! Whoa!

64

Verse

Ride away on your horses,
Your horses, your horses.
Ride away on your horses,
Ride on, ride on.
Galloping, galloping,
  galloping, galloping,
On we go, oh;
Ride away on your horses,
Your horses, your horses.
Ride away on your horses,
Now Whoa! Whoa! Whoa!

Ride-o

Ride-o, ride-o, ride-o, U-pon your horse a-stride-o.

Which way shall we ride-o? To the coun-try-

side-o, To find a pret-ty bride-o.

Verse

Ride-o, ride-o, ride-o,
Upon your horse a-stride-o.
Which way shall we ride-o?
To the countryside-o,
To find a pretty bride-o.

Ride on Daddy's Knee

Ride   on   Dad - dy's   knee,   dear,   And

see   what you   can   see, dear. The cows are in   the

clo - ver. The pigs have gone   to Dov - er.

Verse 1

Ride on Daddy's knee, dear,
And see what you can see, dear.
The cows are in the clover.
The pigs have gone to Dover.

Verse 2

Ride on Daddy's back, dear,
And give the whip a crack, dear.
Around the table and dining chairs
And then we'll ride to bed upstairs.

Riding Here to Get Married

Rid - ing here to get mar - ried, Get mar - ried, get

mar - ried.   Rid - ing   here   to   get   mar - ried,

Ran - som a tan - som a cin - na - mon tea.

Verse

Riding here to get married,
Get married, get married.
Riding here to get married,
Ransom a tansom a cinnamon tea.

Riding in a Buggy

Rid - ing in a bug - gy Miss Mar - y Jane, Miss

Mar - y Jane, Miss Mar - y Jane. Rid - ing in a

bug - gy Miss Mar - y Jane, I'm a long ways from home.

Verse

Riding in a buggy Miss Mary Jane,
Miss Mary Jane, Miss Mary Jane.
Riding in a buggy Miss Mary Jane,
I'm a long ways from home.

This Is the Way...

This Is the Way the Ladies Ride

This is the way the ladies ride,
A clippety-clop, a clippety-clop
And a clippety, clippety, clippety-clop.

This is the way the gentlemen ride,
A gallop-a-trot, a gallop-a-trot
And a gallop, a gallop, a gallop-a-trot.

This is the way the farmers ride,
A hobblety-hoy, a hobblety-hoy
And a hobblety, hobblety, hobblety-hoy!

This is the way the soldiers ride,
With a hep 2, 3, 4, a hep, 2, 3, 4
And a heppety, heppety, hep, 2, 3, 4!

This is the way the cowboys ride,
A whoopy-i-ay, a whoopy-i-ay
And a whoopy, a whoopy, a whoopy-i-ay!

Variation 1

This is the way the ladies ride,
Neat and small, neat and small.

This is the way the gentlemen ride,
Boots and all, boots and all.

This is the way that <u>baby</u> rides,
substitute baby's name
Hurrah, hurrah, hurrah!

Variation 2

This is the way the ladies ride,
Nimble, nimble, nimble, nimble.

This is the way the gentlemen ride,
A gallop, a gallop, a gallop, a trot.

This is the way the farmers ride,
Jiggety jog, jiggety jog.

Variation 3

This is the way the ladies ride,
Prim, prim, prim, prim.

very gentle bounce

This is the way the gentlemen ride,
Trim, trim, trim, trim.

slightly larger bounce

This is the way the hunters ride,
A gallop, a gallop, a gallop, a gallop.

larger bounce

This is the way the farmers ride,
A trot, a trot, a trot, a trot.

very large bounce

This is the way the plough boys ride,
Hobble-dee-gee, hobble-dee-gee.

large bounce from knee to knee

Variation 4

This is the way the ladies ride,
Saddle aside, saddle aside.

bounce baby sitting sideways

This is the way the gentlemen ride,
Saddle astride, saddle astride.

bounce baby straddling your legs

This is the way the babies ride,
Tucked inside, tucked inside.

hug baby

This is how they all looked great
As they all jumped over the ten-bar
gate.

*bounce baby on one knee and at the end lift
baby over the other knee*

Variation 5

This is the way the ladies ride,
Trit, trit, tree; trit, trit, tree;
trit, trit, tree!

This is the way the gentlemen ride,
Gallop-a-trot, gallop-a-trot,
gallop-a-trot!

This is the way the farmer rides,
Hobbledy-hoy, hobbledy-hoy and
down into the ditch!

And when they come to a hedge,
They jump over!

lift baby to other knee

When they come to a slippery place,
They scramble, scramble,
Tumble-down Dick.

slide baby down your leg

This is the Way the Lady Rides (Variation 6)

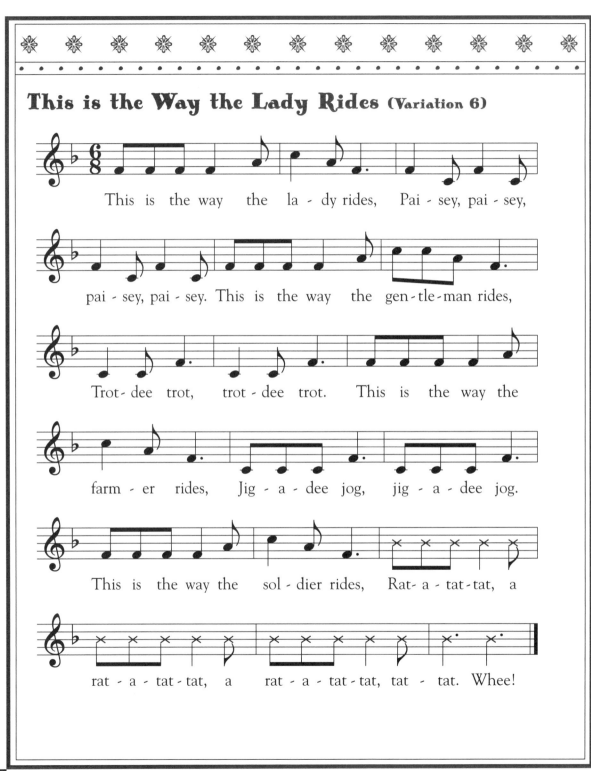

This is the way the la - dy rides, Pai - sey, pai - sey,

pai - sey, pai - sey. This is the way the gen - tle - man rides,

Trot - dee trot, trot - dee trot. This is the way the

farm - er rides, Jig - a - dee jog, jig - a - dee jog.

This is the way the sol - dier rides, Rat - a - tat - tat, a

rat - a - tat - tat, a rat - a - tat - tat, tat - tat. Whee!

Verse

This is the way the lady rides,
Paisey, paisey, paisey, paisey.

This is the way the gentleman rides,
Trot-dee trot, trot-dee trot.

This is the way the farmer rides,
Jig-a-dee jog, jig-a-dee jog.

This is the way the soldier rides,
Rat-a-tat-tat, a rat-a-tat-tat,
   a rat-a-tat-tat, tat-tat. Whee!

So Fahren die Damen
(This Is the Way the Ladies Ride) (Variation 7) *German*

So fah - ren die Da - men, so fah - ren die Da - men, So

rei - ten der Her - ren, so rei - ten der Her - ren, So

blit - zen die Bu - ben, so blit - zen die Bu - ben, So

blit - zen die Bu - ben und fal - len da - hin!

Verse

So fahren die Damen,
  so fahren die Damen,
So reiten der Herren,
  so reiten der Herren,
So blitzen die Buben,
  so blitzen die Buben,
So blitzen die Buben
  und fallen dahin!

Translation:

This is the way the ladies ride,
  this is the way the ladies ride.
This is the way the gentlemen ride,
  this is the way the gentlemen ride.
Like lightning the boys ride,
  like lightning the boys ride.
Like lightning the boys ride
  and fall there!

This Is the Way the Ladies Go (Variation 8)

This is the way the ladies go,
Nimble, nimble, nimble.

This is the way the gentlemen go,
Trot, trot, trot.

But the lord behind
  who drinks the wine goes
Gallopy, gallopy, gallopy
Over the stiles!

This Is the Way the Baby Rides (Variation 9)

This is the way the baby rides,
Baby rides, baby rides.
This is the way the baby rides,
Bouncy, bouncy, bouncy.

bounce slowly

This is the way the jockey rides,
Jockey rides, jockey rides
This is the way the jockey rides,
Gallopy, gallopy, gallopy.

bounce quickly

Here Comes My Lady (Variation 10)

Here comes my lady
  with her little baby,
A nim, a nim, a nim.

Here comes my lord
  with his trusty sword,
A trot, a trot, a trot.

Here comes old Jack
  with a broken pack,
A gallop, a gallop, a gallop.

Here Goes My Lord (Variation 11)

Here goes my lord;
A trot, a trot, a trot, a trot.

Here goes my lady;
A canter, a canter, a canter, a canter.

Here goes my young master;
Jockey-hitch, jockey-hitch,
  jockey-hitch, jockey-hitch.

Here goes my young miss;
An amble, an amble,
  an amble, an amble.

The footman lags behind
  to tipple ale and wine
And goes gallop, a gallop, a gallop
To make up his time.

We Bounce Up

all of these bounces ask you to lift baby into the air at some point

Rub-a-Dub-Dub

Rub-a-dub-dub
Three men in a tub.
And how do you think they got there?
They wiggled and sniggled
And moved very close,
Then jumped up into the air.

lift baby up high

Rocky Horsey

Rocky horsey, rocky horsey
Go to town;
To get some meal,
To make some mush,
To make this baby
Go hush, hush, hush.

lift baby into the air or gently lower baby between legs

Handy Dandy

Handy, dandy riddley ro,
Which will you have,
High or low?

lift baby up high or gently drop baby

between legs

Icky Bicky

Icky bicky, soda cracker,
Icky bicky boo.
Icky bicky, soda cracker,
Up goes you.

lift baby up high

Riddle Me

Riddle me, riddle me, riddle me ree,
Perhaps you can tell
  what this riddle may be.
As deep as a horse,

lay baby back

As round as a cup,

wiggle baby back and forth

And all the king's horses
  can't draw it up.

lift baby up high

(answer: a well)

Dickery Dickery Dare

Dickery, dickery dare,
The pig flew up in the air.

lift baby up high

The man in brown
Soon brought him down.

hold still for a moment

Dickery, dickery dare.

Rigadoon

Rigadoon, rigadoon,
Now let him fly,
Sit him on father's foot,
Jump him up high!

lift baby up high

Zoom

Zoom—, ba, ba, Mommy's baby,

give baby an extra high bounce on "Zoom"

Zoom—, ba, ba, Mommy's baby.
Cover him/her up,
  pat him/her on the head.
Give him/her a little kiss
  and put him/her to bed.

kiss baby's forehead and lay him/her

backwards on your legs

Trot Little Pony

Trot little pony
Down to town.
One foot up

bounce extra high

And the other foot down.

slide baby down your legs

Two Fat Sausages

Two fat sausages
In a frying pan.
One went POP!

lift baby up high

The other went BAM!

lower baby

Put the Oil in the Pot

You put the oil in the pot
And you let it get hot.
You pour the popcorn in
And you start to grin.
Sizzle, sizzle, sizzle, sizzle, POP!

lift baby up high

Bossy-Cow

Bossy-cow, bossy-cow, where do you lie?
In the green meadow under the sky.

slow bounce

Billy-horse, billy-horse, where do you lie?
Out in the stable with nobody nigh.

faster bounce

Birdies bright, birdies sweet,
  where do you lie?
Up in the treetops, oh, ever so high!

lift baby up high

Baby dear, baby love, where do you lie?
In my warm crib, with Mamma close by.

slower bounce ending with a hug

Old Dan Tucker

Old Dan Tucker went to town
Riding a billy goat, leading a hound.
The hound did bark, the goat did jump,
Old Dan Tucker straddled a stump.

lift baby up high

Variation

Buster Brown went to town,
Riding a billy goat,
Leading a hound.
Hound barked, billy goat jumped,
And threw Buster Brown
Right over a stump!

slide baby down your legs

We Bounce Down

unless instructed otherwise, gently drop baby between legs at the end of each rhyme

One to Make Ready

One to make ready,
And two to prepare,
Good luck to the rider
And away goes the mare.

very fast bounces

Thistle-Seed

Thistle-seed, thistle-seed,
Fly away, fly.
The hair on your body
Will take you up high.
Let the wind whirl you
Around and around,
You'll not hurt yourself
When you fall to the ground.

Five Little Riders

Five little riders on a nice fall day,
Jumped on their ponies
  and rode far away.
They galloped in the meadow
And they galloped up a hill.
They galloped so fast
That they all took a spill.

Hold My Bonnet

Hold my bonnet
And hold my shawl
And I'll make Glory hump!*

"Hump" means to get going and not lie around.

Hokey, Pokey

Ho - key,   po - key,   pen - ny   a   lump,

That's the stuff to   make you jump.   If   you jump you're

sure to fall,   Ho - key, po - key,   that's it   all.

Verse

Hokey, pokey, penny a lump,
That's the stuff to make you jump.
If you jump you're sure to fall,
Hokey, pokey, that's it all.

Stacha Minacha *Northern Italian*

Sta - cha Min - a - cha, Ba - bo di - ra co - cha,

Co - cha del bu bu. Me - lé bam - bi - no but - ta ju.

Verse

Stacha Minacha,
Babo dira cocha,
Cocha del bu bu.
Melé bambino butta ju.

gently drop baby between legs

General Translation:

Yoo hoo,
Father went hunting.
When hunting you might get hurt.
My little baby fell down.

the book of bounces

This Is Bill Anderson

This is Bill Anderson.

with baby on your lap, hold one foot in each hand

That is Tom Sim.

on each line, alternate crossing baby's legs one over the other, faster and faster

Tom went to fight,
And fell over him.
Bill over Tom,
And Tom over Bill.
Over and over as
They fell down the hill!

gently drop baby between legs

Whoever Took My Big Black Dog

Whoever took my big black dog,
I wish they would bring him back!
He chased the big chicks
  over the fence,
And the little chicks through the crack.

gently lower baby between legs

Two Little Horses

Two little horses
Went to town.
One went up
And the other went down.

Two in a Hammock

Two in a hammock
Just about to kiss,
When all of a sudden
The darn thing slipped!

slide baby down your leg

Trot Little Horsey

Trot little horsey
Going downtown.
Come to the bridge
And the bridge falls down.

Toffee Little Girl

Toffee little girl to
Toffee town,
Watch out little girl,
Horsey fall down.

Ride a Little Horsey, But Don't Fall Down!

Ride the Little Horsey

Ride the little horsey,

with legs crossed, bounce baby on one foot

Go to mill.
Up the road
And down the hill.

uncross legs and gently drop baby to the floor

Riding in a Cart

Riding in a cart
To visit Farmer Brown.
Whoops, the wheel breaks
And the cart falls down!

Ride a Little Horsey

Ride a little horsey
Down to town.
He don't mind me;
He'll fall down. Whoops!

Variation 1

Ride a little horsey
Down to town.
You better be careful
So you don't fall down.

Variation 2

Ride a horse, ride a horse,
Ride a horse to town.
Ride a horse, ride a horse,
Whoops! - fall down!

Ride a Little Horsey (Variation 3)

Ride a lit - tle hors - ey Up and down. Take
care lit - tle hors - ey So you don't fall down.

Verse

Ride a little horsey
Up and down.
Take care little horsey
So you don't fall down.

We Bounce Around!

all of the bounces in this section vary in tempo or ask you to do different things during the course of the rhyme

Darby and Joan

Darby and Joan were dressed in black,

bounce baby on one knee

Sword and buckle behind their back.
Foot for foot and knee for knee,
Turn about, Darby's company.

bounce baby on other knee

Here We Go Up, Up, Up

Here we go up, up, up.

with legs crossed, baby rides on foot, each bounce higher

Here we go down, down, down.

each bounce lower

Here we go forward,

Here we go backward,

swing leg forward and backward

Here we go around and around.

move leg in circular motion

Gregory Griggs

Gregory Griggs, Gregory Griggs

sit on floor with legs extended; bounce baby while he/she straddles legs

Had twenty-seven different wigs.
He wore them up, he wore them down

lift knees especially high then lower them again

To please the people of the town.

continue bouncing

He wore them east, he wore them west

lean baby to the left, then to the right

And never could tell which he liked best.

continue bouncing

Bimbo, Bimbo

Bimbo, Bimbo,

bounce baby on knees while holding baby's hands

Where you gonna go-e-o?
Bimbo, Bimbo,
What are you gonna do-e-o?
Bimbo, Bimbo,
Who are you gonna see?

slowly lift baby's hands over head

Gonna see baby riding on a pony!

lower baby's hands and bounce twice as fast

Jack Be Nimble

Jack be nimble,
Jack be quick,
Jack, jump over the candlestick.

switch baby from one knee to the other on the word "over"

Little White Ponies

Little white ponies are tied in a barn.
They want to go out to play.
Now watch and they will hop over
the stile

lift baby from one knee to the other

And gallop and gallop away.

bounce a little faster

Hickory, Dickory, Sacra Down!

Hickory, dickory, sacra down!
How many miles to Richmond town?
Turn to the left

lean baby to the left

And turn to the right

lean baby to the right

And you may get there by Saturday
night.

Charley Barley

Charley, barley, buck and rye,

bounce baby on one knee

What's the way the Frenchmen fly?
Some fly east and some fly west

lift baby over onto the other knee

And some fly over the cuckoo's nest.

Humpty Dumpty

Humpty Dumpty sat on a wall.

sit on the floor with knees extended in front

while bouncing baby

Humpty Dumpty had a great fall.

gently straighten legs

All the king's horses
  and all the king's men

gently bounce baby

Couldn't put Humpty together again.

Hey Diddle, Diddle!

Hey diddle, diddle!
The cat and the fiddle,
The cow jumped over the moon.

lift baby from one knee to the other knee

The little dog laughed
  to see such sport
And the dish ran away with the spoon.

Oh, the Noble Duke of York

Oh,   the   No - ble   Duke   of   York,   He

had ten thou - sand   men.   He marched them   up   to the

top   of the hill and he marched them down   a - gain.

Verse 1

Oh, the Noble Duke of York,
He had ten thousand men.
He marched them up
  to the top of the hill
  lift baby high
And he marched them down again.
  lower baby

Verse 2

'Cause when you're up, you're up
  lift baby high
And when you're down, you're down;
  lower baby
But when you're only halfway up,
  lift baby halfway
You're neither up
  lift baby high
Nor down!
  lower baby

the book of bounces

Leg Over Leg

Leg over leg
As the dog went to Dover.
When he got there,
Whoops! He went over.

one large bounce switching baby from one knee
to the other on the word "whoops"

Variation 1

Leg over leg
As the dog goes to Dover.
When he comes to a wall,
Jump! He goes over!

one large bounce switching baby from one knee
to the other on the word "jump"

Variation 2

Leg over leg
As the dog went to Dover.
When he came to a stile,
Jump! He went over!

one large bounce switching baby from one knee
to the other on the word "jump"

Old Farmer Giles

Old Farmer Giles,

start the bounce on one knee

He went seven miles
With his faithful dog, Old Rover.

Old Farmer Giles,
When he came to the stiles,
Took a run and then jumped clean
over.

an extra high bounce to the other knee

Father and Mother and Uncle John

Father and Mother and Uncle John,
All rode to market upon a white ram.
Off fell Father and off fell Mother

lean baby to one side and then to the other

And away rode Uncle John.

bounce a little faster

Variation

Mother and Father and Uncle John
Went to market one by one.
Mother fell off!

lean baby to one side

And Father fell off!

lean baby to the other side

But Uncle John went on
and on and on ...

bounce faster and faster

See the Pony Galloping

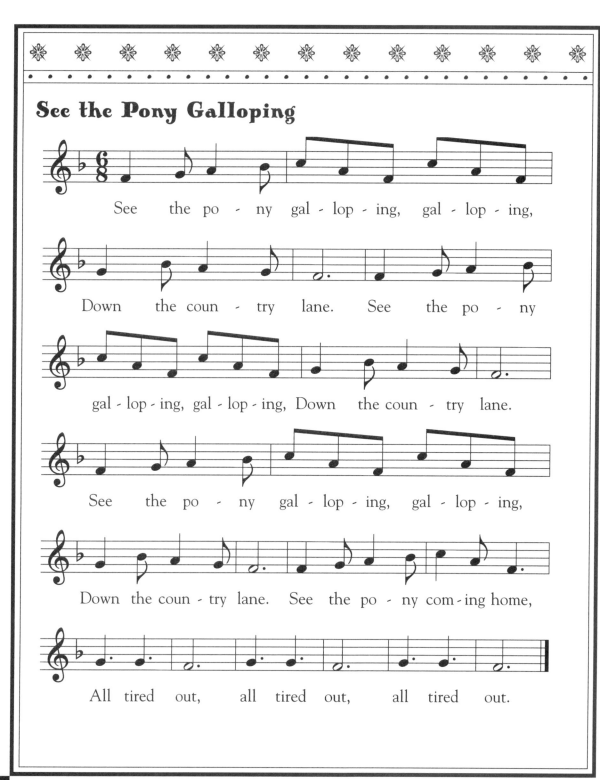

See the po - ny gal - lop - ing, gal - lop - ing,

Down the coun - try lane. See the po - ny

gal - lop - ing, gal - lop - ing, Down the coun - try lane.

See the po - ny gal - lop - ing, gal - lop - ing,

Down the coun - try lane. See the po - ny com - ing home,

All tired out, all tired out, all tired out.

Verse

See the pony galloping, galloping,
Down the country lane.

bounce a little faster

See the pony galloping, galloping,
Down the country lane.

bounce faster still

See the pony galloping, galloping,
Down the country lane.

very fast bounces

See the pony coming home,

slower and slower bounces

All tired out, all tired out, all tired out.

The Huntsman

The huntsman rides a black horse,
bounce on left knee
The soldier rides a gray.
bounce on right knee
To plough and sow and reap and mow,
bounce on left knee
To come and go and whoop and whoa,
bounce on right knee
I'll buy a bonny bay.
lift baby up in the air

Triddety Trot to Market

Triddety trot to market
bounce baby on one knee
To buy a loaf of bread.
Triddety trot and home again
And throw him/her in the bed.
lift baby up and onto other knee

Triddety trot to market
To buy a pat of butter.
Triddety trot and home again
And throw him/her in the gutter.
lift baby up and onto other knee

Trotty Horsey

Trotty horsey, trotty horsey,
Went to town.
One foot up and the other went
Boobaty, boobaty,
    boobaty, boobaty, boo!
lift baby from one knee to the other

The Doggies Went to the Mill

The doggies went to the mill,
place baby on your knees, lifting alternate knees
This way and that way.
The doggies went to the mill,
This way and that way.
They took a lick
    out of this wife's poke,*
lean baby to the right
They took a lick
    out of that wife's poke,
lean baby to the left
And a lap in the lake
    and a dip in the dam
lean baby to the right, then left
And went walloping, walloping,
    walloping ham.
bounce faster and faster
"Poke" is old English for bag or sack.

Tommy O'Flynn

Tom-my O'-Flynn and his old gray mare Went

off to see the coun - ty fair. The

bridge fell down And the bridge fell in And

that was the end of Tom-my O'-Flynn. O'-

Flynn, O'-Flynn, O'-Flynn, O'-Flynn.

Verse

Tommy O'Flynn and his old gray mare
Went off to see the country fair.
The bridge fell down

gently dip baby between your legs

And the bridge fell in,

gently dip baby between your legs

And that was the end
of Tommy O'Flynn.
O'Flynn, O'Flynn, O'Flynn, O'Flynn.

bounce baby faster and faster

Two Little Ponies

Two little ponies riding to town;
hold onto baby's feet while baby is lying on his/her back
Now they go up, now they go down.
lift feet up and then down
This little pony we will call Jack.
bounce one foot up and down
Five little boys are riding on his back.
This little pony I think is called Queen.
bounce the other foot up and down
Five little girls on her back are seen.
"Get up, little ponies, gallop away
bounce both feet up and down
With your little riders so glad today."

Walk Old Joe

Walk Old Joe, walk Old Joe,
You walk better than any horse I know.
slow bounce on one knee

Trot Old Joe, trot Old Joe,
You trot better than any horse I know.
faster bounce on the other knee

Gallop Old Joe, gallop Old Joe,
You gallop better than any horse I know.
baby on both knees, quickly alternate lifting knees
Whoa!
lean back

More Bounces...

An Apple for a King

An apple for a King,
A pear for a Queen
And a good bounce over
The bowling green.

Hey Diddle Dinky

Hey diddle dinky, poppety, pet,
The merchants of London,
  they wear scarlet.
Silk on the collar and gold on the hem,
So merrily march the merchant men.

Up and Down Again

Up and down again
Upon the counterpane,
High and dry and steady.
Baby rides on Mammy's knee
Until her breakfast is ready.

Then she has her pap
On her Daddy's lap,
Warm and snug and cozy.
If she's good and takes her food,
She'll grow up fat and rosy.

Here I Am

Here I am, Jumping Joan.
When nobody's with me,
I'm all alone.

Bee-Dee-Um

Bee - dee-um   bum   bum,   bee - dee-um   bum,

Here   comes   the   man   with   the   man - do - lin.

Bee - dee-um   bum   bum,   bee - dee-um   bum,

Fine

He'll   be   there   when   the   ship   comes   in!

Nice   old   fel - low   sing - in'   a   song,

D.S. al Fine

He   comes   a - round   in   the   af - ter - noon.

Verse

Bee-dee-um bum bum, bee-dee-um bum,
Here comes the man with the mandolin.
Bee-dee-um bum bum, bee-dee-um bum,
He'll be there when the ship comes in!

Nice old fellow singin' a song,
He comes around in the afternoon.
Bee-dee-um bum bum, bee-dee-um bum,
He'll be there when the ship comes in!

Bouncing Up and Down

Bounc - ing up and down in a lit - tle red wag - on,

Bounc - ing up and down in a lit - tle red wag - on,

Bounc - ing up and down in a lit - tle red wag - on,

Won't you be my dar - ling?

Verse 1

Bouncing up and down
  in a little red wagon,
Bouncing up and down
  in a little red wagon,
Bouncing up and down
  in a little red wagon,
Won't you be my darling?

Verse 2

One wheel's off
  and the axle's draggin',
One wheel's off
  and the axle's draggin',
One wheel's off
  and the axle's draggin',
Won't you be my darling?

Dance a Baby Diddy

Dance a ba - by did - dy, What can mam - my do

wid' - e? Sit in her lap, give it some pap,

And dance a ba - by did - dy.

Verse

Dance a baby diddy,
What can mammy do wid'e?
Sit in her lap, give it some pap,
And dance a baby diddy.

Dance to Your Daddy

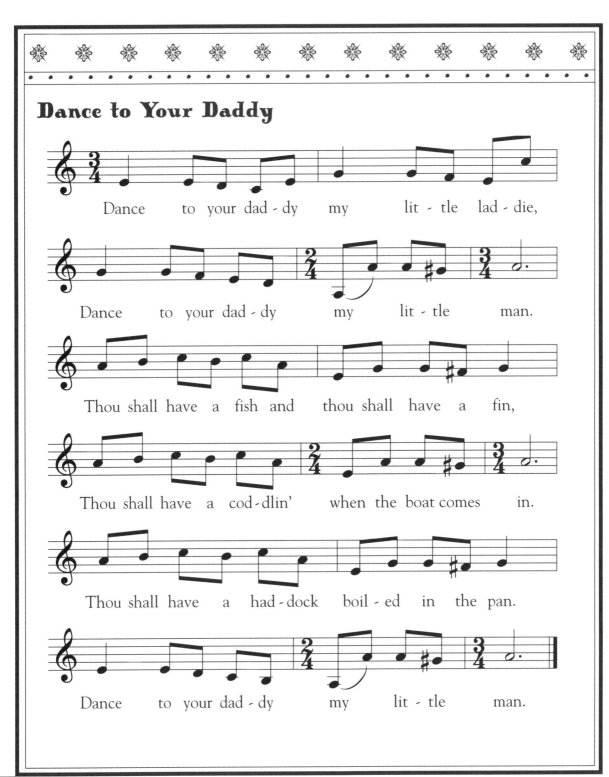

Dance to your dad - dy my lit - tle lad - die,

Dance to your dad - dy my lit - tle man.

Thou shall have a fish and thou shall have a fin,

Thou shall have a cod - dlin' when the boat comes in.

Thou shall have a had - dock boil - ed in the pan.

Dance to your dad - dy my lit - tle man.

Verse

Dance to your daddy my little laddie,
Dance to your daddy my little man.

Thou shall have a fish
  and thou shall have a fin,
Thou shall have a coddlin'
  when the boat comes in.

Thou shall have a haddock
  boiled in the pan.
Dance to your daddy my little man.

Dance to Your Daddy-o

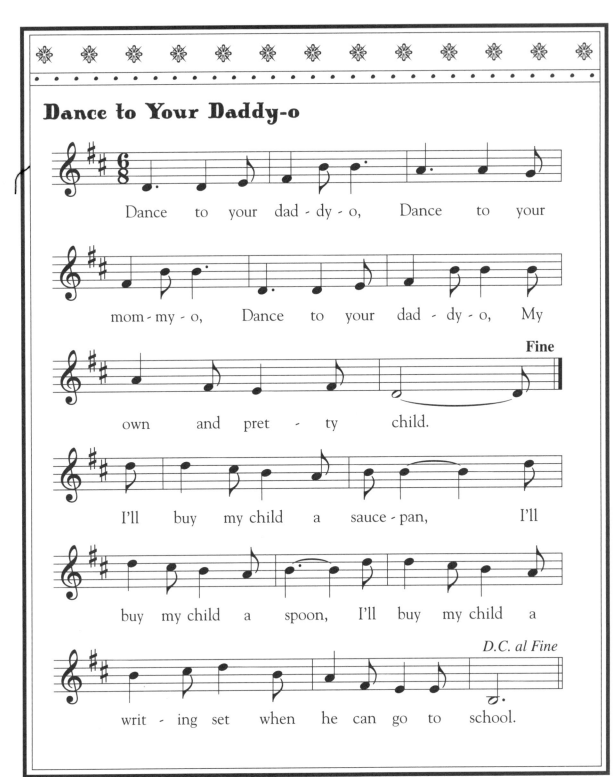

Dance to your dad-dy-o, Dance to your mom-my-o, Dance to your dad-dy-o, My own and pret-ty child.

Fine

I'll buy my child a sauce-pan, I'll buy my child a spoon, I'll buy my child a writ-ing set when he can go to school.

D.C. al Fine

Verse

Dance to your daddy-o,
Dance to your mammy-o,
Dance to your daddy-o,
My own and pretty child.

I'll buy my child a sauce pan,
I'll buy my child a spoon,
I'll buy my child a writing set
When he can go to school.

Dance to your daddy-o,
Dance to your mammy-o,
Dance to your daddy-o,
My own and pretty child.

Dee Um Dum Doo

Dee um dum doo, Dee um dum doo,

Dee um dum doo, Dum-ah Doo-oo Dee-oh.

Verse

Dee um dum doo,
Dee um dum doo,
Dee um dum doo,
Dum-ah Doo-oo Dee-oh.

pull baby close for a snuggle

Halsey, Halsey, Halsey

Hal-sey, Hal-sey, Hal-sey, Hal-sey, O Bob-by Hal-sey,

Hal-sey, Hal-sey, O Bob-by Hal-sey, Hal-sey, Hal-sey, Hey!

Verse

Halsey, Halsey, Halsey, Halsey,
O Bobby Halsey, Halsey, Halsey,
O Bobby Halsey, Halsey, Halsey, Hey!

Here Comes Missis Macaroni

Here comes Miss - is   Mac - a - ro - ni,   Rid - ing on her

milk   white   po - ny,   Here   she   comes   with

all   her   mon - ey,   Miss - is   Mac - a - ro - ni.

Verse

Here comes Missis Macaroni,
Riding on her milk white pony,
Here she comes with all her money,
Missis Macaroni.

Hus Druss Drillyuh (Whoa Slow Down) *German*

Hus druss drill - yuh, John - ny hat ein Fül - len,

Fül - len kann nicht lauf - en, John - ny wills ver - kau - fen.

Verse

Hus druss drillyuh,
Johnny hat ein Füllen,
Füllen kann nicht laufen,
Johnny wills verkaufen.

Translation:

Whoa, Whoa slow down!
Johnny has a foal,
Who cannot run.
Johnny wants to sell him!

My Old Dan

My old Dan is al - ways read - y,

Jog, jog, jog, jog.

Though he is but slow and stead - y,

Jog, jog, jog, jog.

When I want to I can stop him

Just by say - ing, "Whoa! Whoa!"

Verse

My old Dan is always ready,
Jog, jog, jog, jog.
Though he is but slow and steady,
Jog, jog, jog, jog.
When I want to I can stop him
Just by saying, "Whoa! Whoa!"

Index